D0722770

COINS AND MONEY

NICKELS!

ELIZABETH MORGAN

PowerKiDS
press

New York

Published in 2016 by The Rosen Publishing Group, Inc.
29 East 21st Street, New York, NY 10010

First Edition

Editor: Katie Kawa
Book Design: Katelyn Heinle

Photo Credits: Cover, p. 1 (piggy bank) Lizzie Roberts/Ikon Images/Getty Images; cover, pp. 6, 9, 10, 13, 14, 17, 18, 21, 24 (background design element) Paisit Teeraphatsakool/Shutterstock.com; cover, pp. 1, 5, 6, 9, 10, 13, 14, 17, 18, 22 (coins) Courtesy of U.S. Mint; pp. 5, 6, 9, 10, 13, 14, 18, 22 (vector bubbles) Dragan85/Shutterstock.com; p. 5 (girl) DAJ/Getty Images; p. 17 (Thomas Jefferson) John Parrot/Stocktrek Images/Getty Images; pp. 18, 24 (Monticello) Bob Stefko/The Image Bank/Getty Images; pp. 18, 21 (vector bubble) LAN02/Shutterstock.com; pp. 21, 24 (Buffalo nickel) Gregory James Van Raalte/Shutterstock.com; pp. 22, 24 (piggy bank) Ljupco Smokovski/Shutterstock.com.

Library of Congress Cataloging-in-Publication Data

Morgan, Elizabeth.
Nickels! / by Elizabeth Morgan.
p. cm. — (Coins and money)
Includes index.
ISBN 978-1-4994-0735-8 (pbk.)
ISBN 978-1-4994-0733-4 (6 pack)
ISBN 978-1-4994-0501-9 (library binding)
1. Nickel (Coin) — Juvenile literature. I. Morgan, Elizabeth. II. Title.
CJ1836.M674 2016
737.4973—d23

Manufactured in the United States of America

CPSIA Compliance Information: Batch #WS15PK: For Further Information contact Rosen Publishing, New York, New York at 1-800-237-9932

CONTENTS

We can buy things with coins.
A nickel is one kind of coin.

Coins are money made of metal.

One nickel is the same as five cents.

One nickel is the same as five pennies.

Two nickels are 10 cents.
This is the same as one dime.

Five nickels are the same as one quarter. How many cents is that?

Thomas Jefferson is on the front of the nickel. He was the third president of the United States.

The building on the back of the nickel is Thomas Jefferson's home. It is called **Monticello**.

An old kind of nickel had a **buffalo** on it. It was called the Buffalo nickel.

Jordan has eight nickels in his **piggy bank**. How many cents does he have?

WORDS TO KNOW

buffalo

Monticello

piggy bank

INDEX

WEBSITES

Due to the changing nature of Internet links, PowerKids Press has developed an online list of websites related to the subject of this book. This site is updated regularly. Please use this link to access the list: www.powerkidslinks.com/cam/nick